MICHAEL KING

The Depression Workbook for Teens

A Guide to Coping and Healing

Contents

Preface

Approximately 20% of teenagers in the USA experience depression before adulthood.[1] I have extensive experience of working with young people to help them manage their lives, and their work with therapists on supporting them through tough times during their developmental years, and I have felt for a number of years now that there needs to be a single workbook which summarises the key ways in which teens and their families can both understand depression, as well as some of the tips and techniques that can help them manage these difficult times. That is why I have written this book.

The Depression Workbook for Teens is a guide to coping and healing from depression. The workbook is designed for teens aged 13-19, and provides advice on how to identify symptoms of depression, how to cope with them, and how to find treatment. The book also includes exercises that help teens learn how to self-diagnose and treat their depression, as well as tips on social networking and self-care. In my 16 years of practice as a Life Coach I have had the privilege of coaching numerous teenagers who have successfully overcome depression, through a combination of treatments.

The Depression Workbook for Teens is a comprehensive guide to coping and healing from depression. Based on my

---

[1]   https://discoverymood.com/blog/todays-teens-depressed-ever/

interactions and experience of coaching young people, this book provides teens, and their families with the information they need to discover and understand their emotions, find resources to help them cope, and develop healthy behaviors that will support their recovery. The Depression Workbook for Teens is designed as a resource for both teens who are experiencing symptoms of depression and their loved ones who want to support them through this difficult time.

1

What is Depression?

In the United States, depression is one of the most common mental disorders. It is a mood disorder that causes feelings of sadness, emptiness, and hopelessness that can last for weeks or months. Depression can make it difficult to do everyday activities such as eat, sleep, work, or socialize. It can also lead to self-harm. Despite how common depression is, there is still a lot of misunderstanding about it. The first couple of chapters in this book will explain what depression is and how it affects teenagers specifically.

Depression is a mental health disorder that affects millions of people around the world. It can be mild or severe, and it can last for a short period of time or for years. There is no one-size-fits-all answer to the question of how depression affects people, as depression can manifest itself in different ways in different people. However, there are some general signs and symptoms that may indicate that someone is suffering from depression. These include feeling sad or down most of the time, losing interest in things that used to make you happy, experiencing changes in appetite or weight, feeling tired all the time, having difficulty concentrating or making decisions, and feeling suicidal thoughts or behaviors. If you are experiencing any of these symptoms, it is important to seek help from a mental health professional, in addition to reading books such as this one.

Are there different types of depression?

While depression is considered a single disorder, there are actually different types of depression. Knowing the different types can help you get the right treatment.

Major Depression

One in six Americans will experience major depression in their lifetime. It is a serious mental illness that can lead to reduced life chances if left untreated. Major depression is characterized by a persistent feeling of sadness and loss of interest in activities that were once enjoyed. Other symptoms include fatigue, changes in appetite, sleep disturbance, feelings of guilt or worthlessness, and thoughts of death or suicide. The cause of major depression is not fully understood, but it is thought to be caused by a combination of genetic and environmental factors. Treatment for major depression includes medication and therapy.

Dysthymia

Dysthymia is a long-term form of depression that is less severe than major depression. Symptoms usually start in early adulthood and continue for years. People with dysthymia often have trouble functioning at work or school and may have difficulty maintaining relationships.

Seasonal Affective Disorder (SAD)

Seasonal Affective Disorder, also known as SAD, is a mood disorder that affects people during certain times of the year. Most commonly, people experience SAD during the winter months, when there is less natural sunlight. Symptoms can include depression, lack of energy, and problems with concentration. People with SAD often feel better during the spring and summer months. There is no one definitive cause of SAD, but it is believed to be related to changes in light exposure and serotonin levels. There are a number of treatments available for SAD, including light therapy, medication, and counseling.

Postpartum Depression

According to the Centers for Disease Control and Prevention, postpartum depression (PPD) is a mood disorder that can affect women after childbirth. PPD can cause feelings of sadness, anxiety, and emptiness that can last for days, weeks, or months. Symptoms of PPD can interfere with a woman's ability to take care of her baby and herself. This is especially important in the context of young teenage girls who give birth, and may not be aware of PPD (or Post-Natal Depression, as it is also known). Some research suggest that adolescent mothers are more than twice as likely to develop postpartum depression when compared with adult women.[2]

Mild to Moderate Depression

Depression is a common mental illness that affects millions of people each year, and it can cause a wide variety of symptoms, from mild to severe. Mild to moderate depression is the most common type, and it can be treated with medication, therapy, or a combination of the two. This is the largest category of client that I have supported in my coaching, and so I will spend more time focusing on the alleviation of symptoms linked to mild to moderate depression.

It may be helpful to start of with a list of the most common symptoms that are encountered by people who suffer from mild to moderate depression:

- Feeling sad or unhappy most of the time
    - Losing interest in things you used to enjoy

---

[2] See research data here: https://journals.sagepub.com/doi/full/10.1177/11795 56519884042

- Feeling hopeless or pessimistic about the future
- Having problems concentrating or making decisions
- Feeling tired all the time
- Sleeping too much or too little
- Eating more or less than usual
- Feeling restless or irritable
- Thoughts of suicide or self-harm.

Mild depression is a form of depression that does not meet the diagnostic criteria for major depressive disorder (MDD). It is estimated that up to 40% of people who suffer from depression have mild symptoms.

Clinically depressed means that a person has met the diagnostic criteria for depression as outlined in the DSM-5. This means that the person has at least five of the nine symptoms of depression, which can include a loss of interest in activities, feelings of worthlessness or guilt, changes in appetite or sleep habits, difficulty concentrating, persistent thoughts of death or suicide, and physical symptoms such as fatigue or pain.

Moderate depression is different from clinical depression in that it does not meet all of the diagnostic criteria for depression. This means that a person with moderate depression may only have three or four of the nine symptoms of depression. Additionally, people with moderate depression are generally able to carry out their normal activities and responsibilities. These individuals still need support, and moderate depression can also result in clinical/severe depression.

What's it like to have depression?

Depression is a mental illness that can cause people to feel sad, hopeless, and unmotivated for an extended period of time. While everyone experiences sadness or low moods at some points in their lives, when these symptoms are severe and last for weeks or months, it may be indicative of depression. Depression can make everyday tasks such as getting out of bed, showering, or eating seem impossible. It can also lead to thoughts of suicide. Despite common misconceptions, depression is not a personal flaw or a weakness; it is a real medical condition that requires treatment.

How is the experience of depression in the teenage years different from getting depression when you're older?

The experience of depression is different for everyone, depending on a variety of factors such as age, gender, and culture. However, there are some general similarities in the experience of depression among different groups of people. Depression in teenagers is often characterized by feelings of sadness, worthlessness, and hopelessness, while adults with depression may experience more fatigue, sleep disturbances, and changes in appetite. It is also common for teenagers to feel like they are the only ones who are experiencing these symptoms and to feel ashamed or embarrassed about their condition. People I have worked with in the past feel that they are alone, and often feel very lonely in their experience of depression, especially if their friends are continuing with their normal childhood lives, and are unaware of what the sufferer is going through.

Activities on understanding depression

1. Research some teenagers to see how they have managed to overcome their depression.
2. Find out more about each type of depression, and discuss how each type might be experienced by a teenager
3. Are there any aspects that you particularly relate to in this chapter? Why?
4. Summarise the salient points of this chapter onto a note-card.

2

Signs and Symptoms of Depression

Common signs and symptoms of depression

Depression is a mood disorder that causes persistent feelings of sadness and loss of interest in activities. It can lead to a variety of symptoms, both physical and emotional. While everyone experiences some of these symptoms at one time or another, when they are severe and persist for weeks or months, they may be signs of depression.

Some common signs and symptoms of depression include: feeling sad or hopeless most of the time, losing interest in things you once enjoyed, feeling exhausted or having little energy, having problems concentrating or making decisions, feeling irritable or restless, eating more or less than usual, sleeping too much or too little, feeling hopeless and helpless, thinking about suicide or death, and experiencing physical problems such as headaches, stomach aches, and chest pain.

In addition to these, better known symptoms of depression,

there are other, less well known symptoms. I will address some of these in the next section.

Psychotic symptoms of depression

For some people, depression also causes psychotic symptoms, which means that they experience symptoms that are not usually associated with depression.

Psychotic symptoms can include hallucinations (seeing or hearing things that are not really there), delusions (believing things that are not true), and disorganized thinking. These symptoms can make it difficult for people with depression to think clearly, make decisions, and communicate with others.

People with psychotic symptoms may also feel paranoid or suspicious, and may believe that other people are trying to hurt them or control them.

Other aspects to consider

Self-harm and suicide

Depression is a serious illness that can lead to self-harm and suicide. A person with depression is at risk of harming themselves if they feel like there is no other way out. They may also be at risk of suicide if they feel like there is no hope for the future. It is important to seek help from a clinician if you have any of these symptoms.

Commenting on the rising rate of depression in young people (aged 14-17), one study found that rates of depression in young people increased by 60% between the years 2009-2017. Worryingly, suicidal thoughts, and attempts also nearly doubled between 2008 and 2017. This correlation is concerning and even more reason why additional material on this topic is necessary.

If you are feeling suicidal, it is important to get help right away. There are people who can help you through this tough time. You can call a suicide hotline in your area, or go to the emergency room in hospital.

The risk of isolation

Depression can often feel incredibly lonely. The risk of isolation in depression is real; it can lead to a worsening of symptoms and interfere with treatment. There are many reasons why people with depression may isolate themselves. They may feel ashamed, embarrassed, or unworthy of social interaction. They may believe that no one could possibly understand what they're going through. Or they may simply prefer to be alone rather than interacting with others.

Isolation can be very harmful in depression. It can lead to a sense of loneliness and isolation that only makes the symptoms worse. It can also interfere with treatment, making it more difficult to get better.

Research at Brigham Young University suggests that social isolation is not only linked to mental and physical health conditions such as depression, but that being socially isolated is the equivalent risk factor of smoking 15 cigarettes a day.

If you're feeling isolated, it's important to reach out for help. There are many people who want to support you, including family members, friends, therapists, and support groups.

Anxiety in depression

Depression and anxiety often go hand in hand. For people with depression, anxiety can make the symptoms worse. It can be hard to know how to cope with both conditions at the same time. This workbook is designed to help you understand and manage your anxiety while you are working on your depression.

There are a few things that are especially important to keep in mind when you are dealing with anxiety and depression:

1. Don't try to tough it out on your own. It's okay to ask for help from family, friends, or professionals.

2. Be patient with yourself. It takes time to get better, and there will be setbacks along the way.

3. Pay attention to your body and mind. Notice when your anxiety is getting worse, and take steps to deal with it before it gets out of control.

Can depression be a symptom of other mental health problems?

Depression can be a symptom of other mental health problems, such as anxiety disorders, bipolar disorder, or ADHD. When depression is caused by another mental health problem, it is called a secondary depression. Secondary depression is treated with the same methods as primary depression. If you are concerned about whether you have depression or a different mental health issue, you would need to go through and receiving a differential diagnosis, to establish whether you have depression and/or another mental health disorder. To get this done, then please follow your locally approved clinical pathway for diagnosis.

Activities on the signs and symptoms of depression

1. Write down some of the symptoms you/your child have experienced.
2. Find out more about each symptom by researching each one thoroughly.
3. What are the signs and symptoms experienced by other teenagers that you know?
4. Summarise the salient points of this chapter onto a note-card.

3

Causes of Depression

There is no single cause of depression in teenagers. Rather, it is most likely caused by a combination of biological, psychological, and environmental factors. For example, teenage depression may be caused by changes in the brain's chemistry, by stress from family problems or schoolwork, or by negative life events such as the death of a loved one. In this chapter we will cover some of the key biological, psychological and environmental factors that cause depression in teenagers, and how you could work through some of these challenges.

What are the genetic reasons for developing depression?

While the root cause of depression is not fully understood, it is believed that there are a variety of genetic and environmental factors that can contribute to its development.

Some of the genetic factors that may contribute to depression include genes that control serotonin levels[3]. Serotonin is a neurotransmitter that helps regulate mood, and people with low serotonin levels are more likely to experience depression (we will cover serotonin further a little later in this chapter). Additionally, people with certain gene variants are also more likely to develop depression. These gene variants affect the way the brain responds to stress, which can increase a person's risk of developing depression. While genetics certainly play a role in depression, there are many other factors that also contribute to this condition. environmental factors, such as stress or traumatic events, can also trigger or worsen depression. Treatment for depression typically includes medication and therapy, and many people find relief from their symptoms with treatment.

Can teen depression run in families?

While depression can affect anyone, research has shown that there may be a link between teen depression and family history. Some studies suggest that there may be a genetic component to teen depression, meaning that it may run in families. This does not mean that if your parents or grandparents suffered from depression, you will too, but it does indicate that there may be a higher risk for you if other family members have also suffered from the condition.

---

[3] See this article for more information, or for further reading in this area: https://www.ncbi.nlm.nih.gov/pmc/articles/PMC4275332/

Environmental factors

Environmental factors that may contribute to depression include exposure to violence, abuse, or neglect; traumatic life events; and poverty or low socioeconomic status. It's important to note that these are only some of the possible environmental contributors and that each person's experience with depression is unique.

Exposure to violence as a cause of depression

Violence can cause depression in several ways. First, exposure to violence can lead to feelings of fear, anxiety, and insecurity. These feelings can lead to depression. Second, violence can cause physical injuries that may lead to pain and disability. Third, violence can damage relationships and create social isolation. This isolation can lead to depression. Finally, violence can cause psychological trauma that may lead to symptoms of post-traumatic stress disorder (PTSD), which is also associated with depression.

Abuse as a cause of depression

People who have been abused are at an increased risk for developing depression and other mental disorders. Abuse can take many forms, including physical abuse, sexual abuse, emotional abuse, and neglect. It can occur at home, at school, or in other settings. Abuse can have a devastating impact on people's lives and can lead to a variety of psychological problems, including depression.

Traumatic life events as a cause of depression

Some experts believe that traumatic life events can be a cause of depression. Traumatic life events are experiences that are so stressful or overwhelming that they can cause physical and emotional damage. Examples of traumatic life events include: the death of a loved one, a serious illness or injury, domestic violence, and being in a natural disaster. It is believed that traumatic life events can cause depression by disrupting the normal balance of hormones and chemicals in the brain.

Other factors

What are the hormonal reasons for developing depression?

While depression is often seen as a purely psychological disorder, it is now understood that there are many hormonal reasons for developing depression. One of the most important hormones associated with depression is serotonin. Serotonin is responsible for mood, sleep, and appetite, and when levels are low, it can lead to depression. Serotonin is a neurotransmitter that is responsible for mood, appetite, and sleep. It has been found that serotonin levels are lower in people with depression. There are many theories as to why this might be, but the role of serotonin in depression is still being studied. Some medications used to treat depression work by increasing serotonin levels in the brain.

Other hormones that play a role in depression include cortisol and thyroid hormone.

Cortisol is a hormone that is produced by the adrenal gland. Cortisol plays a role in regulating mood, stress, energy levels, and the immune system. When cortisol levels are high, it can lead to anxiety and depression. Studies have shown that people with depression have higher cortisol levels than people without depression. There are treatments available for depression that can help to lower cortisol levels. Thyroid dysfunction is one of the most common medical conditions in the world, and it is estimated that around 30% of people with thyroid dysfunction also have some form of depression. Studies have shown that treating the thyroid dysfunction can improve the symptoms of depression. However, more research is needed to determine the role of thyroid dysfunction in depression.

Activities on the causes of depression

1. Write down some of the causes of depression that you feel most relate to you/your child.
2. Find out more about each cause of depression by selecting one area, and researching that area more thoroughly.
3. What are the causes of other teenage depression experiences that you may have either come across personally, or from research?

4. Summarise the salient points of this chapter onto a note-card.

4

Treatments for Depression

There are many treatments for depression. The most common treatments are antidepressant medications, psychotherapy, and cognitive-behavioral therapy (CBT). Other treatments include electroconvulsive therapy (ECT), transcranial magnetic stimulation (TMS), and light therapy.

Medication

Antidepressant medicine is a type of medication that is used to treat people who are suffering from depression. There are many different types of depression medicine, and they all work in different ways[4]. Some people wonder if depression medicine works for teen depression. There is no one-size-fits-all answer

---

[4] One of the most common type of antidepressant drugs are Selective Serotonin Reuptake Inhibitors (SSRIs). You can find out more about them here: https://www.nhs.uk/mental-health/talking-therapies-medicine-treatments/medicines-and-psychiatry/ssri-antidepressants/overview/

to this question, as the effectiveness of depression medicine will vary from person to person. However, many studies have shown that antidepressant medications can be effective in treating teen depression. In fact, antidepressants are the most commonly prescribed medications for teens with mental health disorders.

There are some potential risks associated with using antide-pressants for teens, but these risks should be weighed against the potential benefits of taking the medication. Overall, it appears that antidepressants can be helpful in treating teen depression, but they should always be used under the guidance of a doctor.

While medication can be beneficial for some people, it is not necessary for everyone. There are many different treatments for depression, including therapy, lifestyle changes, and self-care. If medication does not seem to be helping, it is important to talk to your doctor about other options.

The role of Psychotherapy and other talking-therapies

Psychotherapy is a treatment for mental illness that involves talking to a mental health professional. It can be used to treat depression, anxiety, and other mental health disorders. Psychotherapy can help people understand their thoughts and feelings, deal with stress, and cope with difficult situations. It can also help them develop better coping skills and improve relationships, and can be very helpful for teenagers who are struggling with depression.

CBT or cognitive behavioral therapy is a type of talk therapy that has been shown to be effective in the treatment of depression. CBT for teenage depression helps the teenager learn how to identify and change negative thoughts and behaviors that may be contributing to their depression.

There are many ways in which CBT can help teenage depression. For example, CBT can help teens become more aware of their thoughts and feelings, learn how to cope with difficult emotions, and develop problem-solving skills. CBT can also help teens learn how to set realistic goals and expectations for themselves, and develop healthy coping mechanisms for dealing with stress and setbacks. Below we will explore further some of the ways in which CBT supports people with depression:

A. Exposing and Refuting Cognitive Distortions

Cognitive distortions are inaccurate and irrational thoughts that people often use to make themselves feel worse. They can be very damaging and lead to a lot of suffering. There are several different types of cognitive distortions, but some of the most common ones are:

- *All-or-nothing thinking:* This is when you see things in black-and-white terms, as either good or bad. For example, "I'm a total failure" or "I'm the best person ever."

- *Labeling*: This is when you put a negative label on yourself or someone else. For example, "I'm a screw up" or "He's such a jerk."

- *Mind reading*: This is when you assume you know what someone else is thinking. For example, "She must think I'm so dumb" or "He's not going to like me".

B. Reducing Rumination and Worry

Rumination and worry are common problems for people with depression. They can keep you stuck in negative thoughts and feelings, and make it hard to focus on anything else. Cognitive-behavioral therapy (CBT) is a type of therapy that can help you reduce rumination and worry.

CBT focuses on changing the thoughts and behaviors that contribute to your depression. It teaches you how to identify and challenge negative thoughts, and how to replace them with more positive ones. CBT also teaches skills like problem-solving and relaxation techniques that can help you manage your worries.

If you're struggling with rumination or worry, CBT may be a good option for you. Talk to your therapist about whether it might be helpful for you[5].

---

[5] In the United Kingdom you can access services via the new programme Improving Access to Psychological Therapies (IAPT services).

C. Addressing Behavioural Activation Difficulties

Behavioral activation difficulties are common in people who suffer from depression. People with behavioral activation difficulties may find it hard to get motivated to do anything, even things they enjoy. This can make it difficult to cope with depression. There are a few things that can help people with behavioral activation difficulties.

One thing that can help is setting *small goals.* When people set small goals, it is easier to get started and see progress. This can give them the motivation they need to keep going. It is also important to find activities that are enjoyable and meaningful. Doing things that make us happy can help us feel better mentally and emotionally. Finally, it is important to have a support system in place. Friends and family can provide emotional support and encouragement when needed.

D. Enhancing Social Support

One of the main goals of CBT is to help you become more active and engaged in your life. This may include participating in social activities, such as going out with friends or joining a club. CBT can also help you learn how to better cope with stress and deal with difficult emotions.

If you are struggling with depression, CBT can be a helpful treatment option. In addition to helping improve your mood,

CBT can also help you build up your social support system.

Practicing Mindfulness

Many people with depression find that practicing mindfulness can help lessen their symptoms. Mindfulness is the practice of being aware of your thoughts and feelings in the present moment, without judging them. It can be helpful for people with depression because it allows them to accept their thoughts and feelings without getting wrapped up in them. This can help reduce negative thinking patterns that often contribute to depression.

Mindfulness can also help you focus on the positive aspects of your life, which can be a source of encouragement when you're feeling down. By focusing on the present moment, mindfulness also helps you avoid ruminating on past events or worrying about the future. This can be helpful for people with depression, who are often plagued by negative thoughts.

Finally, mindfulness can help you connect with your body and emotions. When you're depressed, it's common to feel numb or disconnected from your body and emotions.

Other less common treatments for depression

Electroconvulsive therapy

Electroconvulsive therapy (ECT) is a psychiatric treatment in which seizures are induced by passing an electric current through the brain. It is most commonly used to treat severe depression, although it can also be used to treat other mental health conditions. ECT works by altering the levels of neurotransmitters in the brain, thereby restoring balance and relieving symptoms. It is considered one of the most effective treatments for **severe** depression, and has been found to be more effective than antidepressant medications.

Transcranial Magnetic Stimulation (TMS)

The National Institute of Mental Health defines transcranial magnetic stimulation (TMS) as a "noninvasive, outpatient procedure that uses magnetic fields to stimulate nerve cells in the brain." It is used to treat depression, anxiety, and other conditions. TMS therapy uses repeated pulses of magnetic energy to stimulate specific areas of the brain. This stimulation may help improve symptoms in people with depression.

It is not yet clear how TMS works to improve symptoms of depression. Some experts believe that TMS helps to activate or energize certain areas of the brain that may be underactive in people with depression. Others believe that TMS may help to change the way information is processed in these areas, which could lead to improved moods. More research is needed to determine the exact mechanism by which TMS helps improve symptoms of depression.

Activities on the treatments for depression

1. Write down any of the treatments/techniques that you have experience of (if any), and discuss how effective you feel they have been.
2. Find out more about one particular type of treatment by researching it thoroughly.
3. What are the treatment modalities used by other teenagers that you know, from your research? How effective have they been (even anecdotally)?
4. Summarise the salient points of this chapter onto a note-card.

5

Coping with Depression

Self-Help Strategies for Depressed Teens

According to the National Institute of Mental Health, around 7.5 percent of American adults suffer from major depression in a given year. Depressed adolescents are even more common[6]; it's estimated that between 2 and 5 percent of teenagers experience clinical depression. While depression can be a very serious condition, there are many things that depressed teenagers can do to help themselves feel better.

In this chapter I will cover a number of strategies that will

---

[6] Research by Pew shows that American teenage girls are three times more likely than boys to experience depression. So not only is the overall rate of experienced depression increasing amongst young people, but research seems to suggest that this rate of increase is much larger amongst girls. https://www.pewresearch.org/fact-tank/2019/07/12/a-growing-number-o f-american-teenagers-particularly-girls-are-facing-depression/

help support teenagers in their recovery from depression. As discussed in the previous chapter, these strategies are best used in conjunction with support from clinical psychologists and clinicians, especially when the number of symptoms experienced is larger than 2-3 or if self-harming and suicidal thoughts are involved (in which case immediate clinical advice needs to be sought).

Journalling

One great self-help strategy for depressed teens is to keep a journal. Writing down your thoughts and feelings can help you to understand and manage your emotions better. It can also be a helpful way to track your progress over time. Other self-help strategies that may be useful for depressed teens include exercise, relaxation techniques, and positive thinking exercises. We will expand on these techniques in this chapter.

A journal can be a helpful tool for people with depression. It can provide a way to express thoughts and feelings, track progress, and set goals. Journals can also help people connect with others who are going through similar experiences.

Relaxation techniques for depression

While medication and therapy are often effective in treating depression, there are also many relaxation techniques that can help to reduce symptoms. Some relaxation techniques that have been shown to be helpful for people with depression include yoga, meditation, deep breathing exercises, and aromatherapy. We will cover a few of these below:

Yoga

The practice of yoga has long been thought to be a way to improve mental health, and recent studies have shown that it can be an effective treatment for depression[7]. Yoga has been found to help people with depression in a few ways. First, it can help people to develop a more positive self-image. Second, it helps to increase energy and vitality, which can be depleted in people with depression. Third, yoga helps to improve mood by releasing endorphins. Finally, yoga is an effective way to reduce stress, which is often a contributing factor in depression.

Breathing Exercises

When people feel stressed or overwhelmed, they might instinctively hold their breath. This is not the best way to deal with stress, however. Conscious deep breathing can help to calm the mind and reduce feelings of depression.

There are a few different types of deep breathing exercises that can be helpful in reducing depression. The first is diaphragmatic breathing, which involves focusing on drawing air deep into the

---

[7]   https://www.ncbi.nlm.nih.gov/pmc/articles/PMC5871291/

lungs, using the diaphragm muscle. This type of breath helps to oxygenate the blood and release tension in the body.

· *Diaphragmatic breathing*

Diaphragmatic breathing is a technique that helps you use your diaphragm to breathe more deeply and efficiently. When you use your diaphragm to breathe, it increases the amount of air that enters your lungs, which can help improve your oxygen levels and reduce stress. Diaphragmatic breathing also helps promote relaxation and can be a useful tool for managing anxiety or panic attacks.There are several ways to practice diaphragmatic breathing, but one of the most common techniques is to place one hand on your stomach and another hand on your chest. As you inhale, focus on pushing your stomach outwards while keeping your chest still. Exhale slowly and completely, allowing your stomach to fall inward. Repeat this process for several minutes, taking deep breaths and relaxing into the rhythm of your breath.

Another type of deep breathing exercise is alternate nostril breathing. This involves alternately inhaling through each nostril, which can help to balance the left and right hemispheres of the brain. It can also help to calm the mind and relieve stress.

· *Alternate Nostril Breathing*

Alternate nostril breathing, which is also known as *nadi shod-*

hana[8], is a breathing technique that is said to be helpful in calming the mind and balancing the body. The practice involves alternating between breathing through the left and right nostrils. This can be done by using your fingers to close off one nostril at a time, or by using a tool such as a yoga nose plug.

There are many benefits claimed for alternate nostril breathing, including improved mental clarity, reduced stress and anxiety, and better overall health. Some people also find that this type of breathing helps them to fall asleep more easily. There is some scientific evidence to support the use of alternate nostril breathing for improving mental health and reducing stress levels, but more research is needed to confirm these benefits.

Try some of these deep breathing exercises to aid relaxation.

In addition to using relaxation techniques, it is important for people with depression to make sure they are getting enough sleep and exercise, and eating a balanced diet. Taking care of oneself is crucial for managing depression and improving one's mood.

---

[8] To find out more about this technique please see here: https://www.banyan botanicals.com/info/ayurvedic-living/living-ayurveda/yoga/nadi-shodhan a-pranayama/

Positive thinking exercises

People with depression often have a difficult time thinking positively about themselves and their lives. However, there are some things you can do to help yourself think more positively.

One way to start thinking more positively is to practice positive affirmations. Positive affirmations are statements that you repeat to yourself that help you feel good about yourself and your life. Some examples of positive affirmations are: "I am capable and competent," "I am loved and supported," and "I am doing the best I can." Positive affirmations can be used to combat any type of negative thinking, but they are particularly effective in reducing the symptoms of depression.

When used correctly, positive affirmations can help you to change your negative beliefs about yourself and replace them with more positive ones. This can lead to a decrease in depressive symptoms and an overall improvement in your mental health.

Another way to start thinking more positively is to focus on the good things in your life. Every day, make a list of five things that you are grateful for. These can be big things, like your family and friends, or small things, like the sun shining on your face.

Exercise

Exercise is one of the **most effective ways** to reduce depression. When you exercise, your body releases endorphins, which are hormones that make you feel good. Exercise also helps improve your mood by distracting you from negative thoughts and providing a sense of accomplishment. In addition, exercise can improve your sleep quality and increase your energy level.

There is a lot of scientific evidence that shows exercise reduces depression[9]. In fact, according to the Centers for Disease Control and Prevention (CDC), physical activity can be just as effective as antidepressants in reducing symptoms of depression. One study published in the journal Psychiatry Research found that participating in a moderate-intensity aerobic exercise program for eight weeks was just as effective as taking an antidepressant medication in reducing symptoms of depression[10]. And, another study published in the journal Medicine and Science in Sports and Exercise found that people who engaged in regular physical activity had a lower risk of developing depression than those who did not engage in regular physical activity[11].

So, what's the take-home message? If you are struggling with depression, consider adding exercise to your treatment plan. Not only will it help reduce your symptoms, but it will also make you feel better physically and mentally.

Good Nutrition

Good nutrition can also play a role in reducing symptoms. Some foods that may help reduce depression symptoms include omega-3 fatty acids, probiotics, and antioxidants. Omega-3

---

[9]   https://www.ncbi.nlm.nih.gov/pmc/articles/PMC474733/

[10]   https://www.ncbi.nlm.nih.gov/pmc/articles/PMC1470658/

[11]   https://www.kcl.ac.uk/news/engaging-in-physical-activity-decreases-peo ples-chance-of-developing-depression-2

fatty acids are found in fish oil supplements and may help to improve mood by increasing levels of serotonin. Probiotics are beneficial bacteria that are found in yogurt and other fermented foods, and they may help to reduce inflammation and improve mood. Antioxidants are found in fruits and vegetables, and they may help to protect the brain from damage caused by stress.

Let's take a quick look at some of these food groups, and discuss how they help reduce depression symptoms.

· *Omega-3 fatty acids*

Omega-3 fatty acids are found in fish oil supplements and are believed to play a role in reducing inflammation and improving mood. A growing number of studies suggest that omega-3 fatty acids may be helpful for treating depression[12]. For example, one study found that omega-3 supplementation was as effective as antidepressants in reducing symptoms of depression.

Omega-3 fatty acids are thought to work by increasing levels of serotonin, a neurotransmitter that is known to affect mood. They may also help improve communication among brain cells and reduce inflammation.

· *Probiotics*

In recent years, probiotics have been gaining attention as a potential treatment for depression. A growing number of studies

---

[12] https://www.ncbi.nlm.nih.gov/pmc/articles/PMC5481805

suggest that probiotics may be beneficial for reducing symptoms of depression.

One possible mechanism by which probiotics may help to reduce depression is by altering the gut microbiota. The gut microbiota has been shown to play a role in mood and behavior. Probiotics may help to improve mood by increasing the abundance of beneficial bacteria and reducing the abundance of harmful bacteria.

Another possible mechanism by which probiotics may help to reduce depression is by increasing levels of serotonin. Serotonin is a neurotransmitter that is known to play a role in mood. Probiotics may increase levels of serotonin by inhibiting the activity of harmful bacteria that produce substances that interfere with serotonin production.

· *Antioxidants*

Antioxidants are substances that help protect cells from damage caused by harmful molecules called free radicals. Some studies suggest that antioxidants may help reduce the symptoms of depression. One theory is that antioxidants may help improve mood by protecting the brain from damage caused by free radicals.

In addition to eating healthy foods, it is important to avoid foods that can worsen symptoms of depression.

Which foods worsen symptoms of depression?

There are many different foods that are known to worsen the symptoms of depression. Foods that are high in sugar, for example, can cause a person to feel more down in the dumps. This is because sugar can cause a spike in blood sugar levels, which then leads to a crash in energy levels. This can make it difficult for someone to feel motivated or cheerful.

Another food group that is known to worsen symptoms of depression are fatty foods. Foods that are high in unhealthy fats can lead to inflammation in the body, which has been linked with an increased risk of depression. Additionally, these types of foods can slow down digestion and contribute to feelings of bloat and sluggishness.

Finally, caffeine should also be avoided if you are struggling with depression. Caffeine is a stimulant and can make it difficult for someone to relax and sleep well.

The role of social support in treating depression

Depression can be a very isolating experience, but luckily, there are many ways to get the support you need. Friends and family can offer a listening ear and emotional support, which can be very helpful in recovering from depression. Joining a support group or seeing a therapist can also provide social support and help you learn new coping skills.

Depression can be a very isolating experience, but emerging research suggests that having a good social network is vital for positive mental health. A recent study published in the journal JAMA Psychiatry found that people with strong social networks were less likely to develop depression[13]. The study looked at data from more than 34,000 people over the course of eight years. It found that those who had five or more close friends were about half as likely to develop depression as those who had fewer than two close friends.

"Our findings suggest that interventions that promote the development and maintenance of social networks may be beneficial for preventing depression," said study author Dr. William Copeland.

Friendships are an important part of our lives, and it's good to know that they can also play a role in protecting us from mental health problems.

Express your feelings

One of the best ways to cope with depression is to express your feelings. This may include talking to a trusted friend or family member, writing in a journal, or participating in an online support group. By expressing your feelings, you can begin to understand them better and work through them.

---

[13] https://jamanetwork.com/journals/jamapsychiatry/article-abstract/27882
63

Good sleep hygiene

Another key tactic to managing depression is practicing good sleep hygiene. Getting enough sleep is essential for overall physical and mental health. People who are depressed often have trouble sleeping, but making sleep a priority can help improve moods. Some tips for getting a good night's sleep include going to bed and waking up at the same time each day, avoiding caffeine and alcohol before bed, and winding down for 30 minutes before sleep.

- *The role of sleep in regulating our mood*

Sleep is critical for our overall health and well-being. It plays a role in regulating our mood, and when we don't get enough sleep, it can lead to feeling down or depressed. In fact, research has shown that people with insomnia are more likely to suffer from depression than those who get a good night's sleep.

- *How sleep patterns can contribute to depression and depressive symptoms*

Sleep deprivation and irregular sleep patterns are both linked with an increased risk for developing depression. In fact, one study found that people who slept for fewer than six hours per night were about twice as likely to develop depression as those who slept for seven or eight hours.

There are a few possible explanations for why poor sleep can lead to depression. One theory is that lack of sleep can disrupt the balance of certain hormones in the body, including serotonin and cortisol. These hormones play a role in mood and energy levels, so when they're out of balance it can lead to symptoms of depression.

Another possibility is that poor sleep can interfere with the brain's ability to form new memories and learn new things. This can make it harder to cope with stress and manage negative thoughts and emotions.

There are several things you can do to help improve your sleep hygiene and get the most out of your slumber. Establish a regular bedtime routine, avoid caffeine and alcohol before bed, make sure your bedroom is dark and quiet, and practice some relaxation techniques before bedtime. If you continue to have trouble sleeping, talk to your doctor about possible treatment options.

Getting enough sleep is essential for our mental health and wellbeing, and in addition to good sleep hygiene, it is important to seek professional help if depression is impacting daily life. A therapist can provide support and guidance in managing depression symptoms.

Avoid Drugs and Alcohol

Unfortunately, depression can be made worse by drug and alcohol abuse. Drugs and alcohol can worsen the symptoms of depression and make it harder for people to recover from the illness. Substance abuse can also lead to other mental health problems, such as anxiety and addiction.

People with depression should avoid drugs and alcohol. If you are struggling with depression, seek help from a mental health professional.

Remember to Have Fun

Depression can be a difficult thing to cope with, especially when it seems like nothing fun is happening in your life. It's important to find ways to enjoy yourself, even when you don't feel like it. Doing things that make you happy can help you feel better emotionally and physically. Here are some tips for having fun:

- Get involved in activities that interest you. Whether it's painting, hiking, biking, playing a sport, or something else altogether, finding an activity you love will help make being active more enjoyable.
- Connect with friends and family members. Spending time with loved ones can help take your mind off of your troubles and make you feel supported.
- Take some time for yourself.
- Look for new ways to improve your health and fitness.

Activities on coping with depression

1. Write down some of management strategies and techniques that either you have used or find interesting.
2. Discuss how effective they have been in helping alleviate symptoms of depression, or your willingness to try out new strategies.
3. What are the coping methods and management strategies used by other teenagers that you know (or have researched)?
4. Summarise the salient points of this chapter onto a notecard.

6

Cultural and Gender Considerations in Teenage Depression

Gender

D epression is not just a mental health condition – it also has cultural and gender dimensions. For example, in some cultures it is less acceptable for boys or men to express their emotions than girls or women. This can lead to boys and men being less likely to seek help for their depression, which can make the condition worse.

Similarly, girls and women often face different expectations about how they should behave and look. This can add to the pressure they feel if they are struggling with depression. It's important to remember that depression affects people of all genders, cultures, and races. In a previous chapter we discussed how, in recent years, teenage girls in the United States were almost three times more likely than boys to experience depression. Some of these cultural and social factors are likely at play in this disparity.

How gender norms and stereotypes affect depression and depressive symptoms

While depression can affect anyone, it is often more common in women than men. This may be due in part to the way gender norms and stereotypes contribute to increased levels of depressive symptoms in women.

One study found that women are more likely than men to internalize the societal messages that dictate how they should behave and look. This can lead to feelings of shame and worthlessness, which are known risk factors for depression. Additionally, research has shown that when women do not conform to gender-stereotypical behaviors or appearances, they are more likely to experience depressive symptoms.

This suggests that the way we view gender and the expectations we place on people of different genders can have a significant impact on mental health.

Depression in teenage girls

Depression is a serious issue that affects people of all ages. For teenage girls, depression can be especially harmful. Girls who are depressed often have low self-esteem and feel like they are a burden to others. They may also feel guilty, ashamed, and hopeless. Depression can lead to problems in school, with friends, and in relationships.

There are many things that can cause depression in teenage girls. These include family problems, stress from school or work, and relationship issues. Girls may also be more likely to develop depression if they have a history of abuse or if there is a family history of mental health problems.

A recent study found that around 1 in 5 teenage girls experience depression. The study also found that teenage girls who are obese are more likely to experience depression than their thinner peers.

There are many reasons why teenage girls might be more likely to experience depression. Some of the possible factors include hormonal changes, stress from school or social pressure, and traumatic life events. We have covered these potential causes in a previous chapter, and the coping mechanisms will be similar to boys (and these techniques have been covered in the previous chapter).

Technology and Depression

The other aspect that needs to be discussed here is the responsibility of technology companies (apps such as Instagram, TikTok etc) that help amplify inappropriate portrayals of gender norms and appearances.

Technology companies have long been criticized for their role in encouraging and amplifying depression. Many people argue that technology companies, and social media platforms in particular, are responsible for the increasing rates of depression we are seeing today. While it is true that technology can be addictive and isolating, it is also true that it can be a powerful tool for connection and self-expression.

It is important to remember that technology is just a tool. It can be used for good or bad, depending on the person using it. For people who are struggling with depression, technology can be a powerful tool for connection and self-expression. Platforms like Instagram and Facebook can be used to connect with friends and share your thoughts and feelings. Technology can also be used to find support from other people who are struggling with depression.

I believe having a *good balance* is the best approach when it comes to technology, and to limit usage of technology devices regardless of whether you are experiencing depressive symptoms or not.

Cultural factors

Depression is a complex mental health disorder that can be caused by a variety of factors, including cultural influences. For example, in some cultures it is considered shameful to admit that you are experiencing mental health problems, such as depression, so people may not seek help. Additionally, the way that depression is treated can vary depending on the culture. In some cultures, traditional healing methods may be used instead of or in addition to medication and therapy. It is important to understand the cultural influences on depression in order to provide the best possible treatment for teens who are struggling with this condition.

Additionally, cultural factors can influence how people perceive and respond to stressors. This can be seen in the fact that some people tend to cold-shoulder stressors, while others will seek out social support (i.e., other people) to manage stress or cope with a stressful situation.

Depression in The 'West'

Depression has been found to be one of the most common mental health problems in western societies. The prevalence of depression in these societies is high, and it is often left untreated. There are a number of contributing factors to this, including the way that depression is viewed and diagnosed in these cultures.

There are a number of myths and misconceptions about depression that can lead to people not seeking help. For example, many people believe that depression is a character flaw or that it is caused by personal failings. Others may think that they can "snap out" of it if they try hard enough.

Another issue is that depression is often not diagnosed properly or accurately in western societies. This can be due to the way that symptoms are interpreted, or because people do not want to admit that they are struggling.

Depression in The 'East'

Depression is a global problem that affects people from all walks of life. While it is most commonly diagnosed in the western world, it is also prevalent in eastern societies. In some cases, depression may be more prevalent in eastern societies than in the west.

In China, for example, it is the leading cause of disability. The prevalence of depression in other eastern societies ranges from 5% to 20%.

There are various factors that contribute to the high prevalence of depression in eastern societies. One key factor is the traditional belief that mental health problems are a sign of weakness and should be kept secret. This means that people with mental health problems often do not receive the help they need. Additionally, the stigma attached to mental health problems means that many people do not seek treatment even when they do recognize that they have a problem.

Depression and Social Class

Depression can be experienced differently by different social classes. For example, those who are in lower social classes may experience depression as a lack of food, shelter, or money. They may feel like they are stuck in a cycle of poverty and cannot escape. In contrast, those in higher social classes may experience depression as a sense of emptiness or boredom. They may feel like they have everything but are still unhappy. It is important to remember that depression is not specific to any social class and can affect anyone.

Historical Events of Great Change

The period after the First World War saw a rise in the number of people with depression. This was due to many factors, including: an increase in women entering the workforce, changes in family structure, and a breakdown of traditional social structures. In the 1920s, in Great Britain, the first cases of depression were reported. Prior to this time, people would often suffer from symptoms of depression for periods of time but then recover. Depression was likely very under reported prior to the 1920s.

Depression & Ethnicity

There are a number of ways in which ethnicity can affect depression. One way is that some ethnic minorities may face discrimination or racism, which can lead to feelings of isolation and decreased self-esteem. Additionally, some cultures have a higher prevalence of mental health disorders such as depression, and certain beliefs or values about mental health may make it more difficult for people from these cultures to seek help. Finally, access to care, and the cultural competency of service providers, can also be barriers to treatment for those from ethnic minority groups. The ethnicity-specific depression symptoms may differ significantly from person to person. There are also some ethnic groups that have a higher prevalence of mental health disorders than others.

According to the National Institute of Mental Health, in the United States, people of Hispanic descent are twice as likely to experience depression as non-Hispanic whites. African Americans are also more likely to suffer from depression than whites.

There are many possible reasons for this disparity. Racism and discrimination can lead to feelings of isolation and despair, and poverty and unemployment are also major risk factors for depression. Additionally, members of minority groups may not have access to quality mental health care, or they may be reluctant to seek help due to shame or stigma.

Activities on cultural and gender considerations in depression

1. Are there discussions in this chapter that you find interesting? could you pick one and research further. What impact could this knowledge have on your understanding of your own depression (or that of your child/friend/student)?
2. Discuss how this knowledge in this chapter would be helpful in managing your own depression, and how you could alter techniques, understanding and interpretation of events/phenomena so that it would help alleviate symptoms of depression.
3. What would you like to learn more about? Pick an area and extend your understanding of that area further by researching online.
4. Summarise the salient points of this chapter onto a note-card.

7

What can other people do to support teenagers with depression?

What can parents do?

First, it is important for parents to understand what teen depression is and how it differs from typical teenage mood swings. Teen depression is more than just feeling sad or down; it is a persistent state of sadness or low mood that interferes with a teen's ability to function normally. Symptoms of teen depression can include changes in appetite, sleeping habits, energy levels, concentration, and self-esteem. If you are concerned that your teen may be depressed, the best thing to do is talk to them about it. Ask them how they are feeling and whether they have been having any problems at school or with friends.

Depression can be debilitating for anyone, but especially for teenagers who are still trying to figure out who they are and where they fit in the world. While there is no one-size-fits-all answer for how to deal with depression, there are many ways parents can help empower their teen to feel better.

First, it's important for parents to understand that depression is a real illness that should be taken seriously. Don't try to brush it off as a phase or something the teen is doing to get attention. Recognize the symptoms of depression and seek help if needed.

Second, talk openly with your teen about depression and mental health in general. Let them know that it's okay to talk about their feelings, even if they're worried about what you might think.

What can schools do?

There are things educators and schools can do to help alleviate teen depression. One important step is to create a safe and supportive environment for students. This means providing emotional support as well as recognizing and addressing mental health issues. Schools can also promote positive body image and healthy relationships, teaching students how to cope with stress and deal with difficult emotions. By creating a healthy school climate, educators can help set the stage for teens to thrive both academically and emotionally.

First and foremost, it is important to be aware of the signs of depression and be willing to talk openly about mental health with your students. It is also important to create a safe and supportive environment in which students feel comfortable discussing their feelings and asking for help.

What can friends do to alleviate teen depression?

While depression can be a very serious condition that requires professional help to overcome, there are things friends can do to help alleviate the symptoms of depression in teens. First and foremost, friends should be supportive and understanding. Teens often feel isolated and misunderstood, so simply being there for them can make a big difference. Friends can also encourage teens to get involved in activities they enjoy, or to see a therapist if they feel like they need more help. Ultimately, it's important to remember that every person is different and what works for one teen may not work for another. If you're not sure what to do to help your friend who is struggling with depression, just ask them!

Tips & techniques for supporting teenagers with depression

A. *Encourage social connection*

Teens who are depressed often isolate themselves from others, so getting them back into social situations can be very helpful. You can do this by organizing get-togethers with friends or family, or by signing them up for activities they enjoy. It's also important to be supportive and understanding. Let them know that you're there for them, and don't judge them. Teens who are depressed need understanding and support from the people around them in order to get better.

B. Make physical health a priority in depression

Here are some tips for making physical health a priority in depression:

- Get moving! Exercise releases endorphins, which have mood-boosting effects. Even if you don't have the energy to go to the gym or run, try taking a walk around your neighborhood or going for a light jog.
- Eat healthy foods. Eating nutritious foods helps your body feel good both physically and mentally. Make sure to include plenty of fruits and vegetables, whole grains, and lean protein in your diet.

C. Know when to seek professional help

It can be very hard to deal with on your own, which is why it's important to know when to seek professional help.

If you (or your teenage son/friend) are feeling down most of the time and you can't seem to shake it, or if your depression is causing you to have problems in your life, it's probably time to see a therapist. Therapists are trained to help people deal with their depression and they can provide you with the tools and support you need to start feeling better. In countries like the United Kingdom you can access therapists and Cognitive Behavioural Therapy (CBT) through the National Health Service (NHS), so speak to your doctor to see what options are available to you.

If your depression is severe or if it's not getting any better after trying different treatments, then it might be time to consider medication. There are many different medications available that can help reduce the symptoms of depression, so don't be afraid to talk to your doctor about them.

D. Support teenager through depression treatment

For teens, depression can be especially difficult to cope with, as they are still trying to figure out who they are and what they want in life. However, there is help available for teens struggling with depression.

If you are the parent of a teen who is dealing with depression, it is important that you provide them with support throughout their treatment. This includes being there for them when they are feeling down, but also praising them when they make progress. It is also important to be patient; recovery from depression can take time.

E. Take care of yourself (and the rest of the family)

Depression can be a very challenging time for both teens and their families. Here are a few tips for helping everyone stay healthy and supportive during this time:

- Get plenty of rest. When you're supporting someone with depression, it can also be tough to maintain a healthy lifestyle, however it is paramount that you too are ensuring you try to get as much sleep as possible. This will help your body heal and restore itself.
- Eat healthy foods. As you are focusing more on supporting others with depression, its important not to forget about your own nutrition needs, and eating healthy foods will keep your energy levels high throughout this period.
- Exercise regularly. Exercise releases endorphins, which have mood-boosting effects, and this can be as helpful to the caregivers, as it can to those who are themselves exercising to overcome depression and depressive symptoms.
- Spend time with supportive people. Support groups for caregivers and carers are an important way to seek support and sometimes time-out for carers. The more regular downtime a carer can get, the less risk they run of depleting their resources.

F. Involve your child in treatment choices for depression

If you have a child who has been diagnosed with depression, it is important to include them in the treatment decisions. Depression can be a very serious illness, and left untreated, it can lead to other problems, such as drug abuse or self-harm. There are many different treatments for depression, including medication, therapy, and lifestyle changes.

Your child's doctor will probably recommend a combination of treatments. It is important to find the treatment that works best for your child. If one treatment doesn't work, don't be afraid to try something else.

Your child can help by telling the doctor what has worked for them in the past, and by telling the doctor if they are having any side effects from the medication. They can also help by keeping a journal of their moods and symptoms. This can help the doctor determine if the treatment is working or not.

In this chapter I presented some ways in which other people can also support the affected teenager with their depression and depressive symptoms. I hope this chapter has been useful for some ideas through which a collective social system can work together to reduce the current epidemic of teenage depression we are currently facing.

Conclusion

This workbook has been designed to help teenagers through their depressive symptoms. The questions in the book have been created and crafted as a way to aid self-discovery and layered learning about depression and its management. The information in this book can be used to identify and understand the causes of depression, learn how to deal with negative thoughts and emotions, and develop healthy coping strategies. If you are a teenager who is struggling with depression, I hope you have found this book useful, and if you are a parent or educator, I also hope the information presented here has been of help. If you would like to discover some of our other titles then please see our website mentalhealthpublishing.com for more details.

Conclusion